MILE HIGH DENVER

Introducing the Author

Caroline Bancroft has Colorado history in her bones. Her pioneer grandfather, Dr. F. J. Bancroft, for whom Mt. Bancroft was named, founded the Colorado Historical Society. Her father, George J. Bancroft, a mining engineer, wrote extensively on Colorado mining and reclamation affairs for both eastern and western publications.

Miss Bancroft herself is the author of four historically accurate and intensely interesting booklets about Colorado, *"Silver Queen: The Fabulous Story of Baby Doe Tabor," "Historic Central City," "Famous Aspen,"* and *"The Melodrama of Wolhurst."*

For five years Caroline Bancroft edited the book page and wrote a literary column for The Denver Post. She free-lanced her way around the globe, interviewing famous people from London to Calcutta.

Following her graduation from Smith College, she obtained a Master's degree from the University of Denver, with a thesis written about Central City. She is an acknowledged authority on mining folklore, as well as many other aspects of Colorado history. Caroline Bancroft is an ideal person to write about the colorful capital of Colorful Colorado.

Quigg Newton,
Mayor of Denver

MILE HIGH DENVER

Its Complete Story as Guide and Souvenir

by

CAROLINE BANCROFT

✦ ✦ ✦

Illustrated with Photographs
from
The Denver Public Library,
D. L. Hopwood Studio,
Floyd McCall
and
Samuel F. McRae

✦ ✦ ✦

The Golden Press, Denver 15, Colorado
and
The American News Co., New York City
1952

CAPITOL HILL—5,280 FEET HIGH ON THE TOP FLIGHT OF STEPS

As Denver is America's highest metropolis, a bronze plaque marks the exact spot with "One Mile Above Sea Level." Here is the eastern half of the Civic Center. Up Colfax Avenue on the left are the State Office Building, Argonaut Hotel and Immaculate Conception Cathedral. At right

WAY STATION

Denver was founded on a jumped claim.

It happened in November, 1858, less than a hundred years ago. The scene was the prairie wilderness ten miles east of the rampart of the snowy Rockies. Here the expanse was broken by a charming cottonwood grove. Through the trees straggled a wide sandy creek bed, moistened by criss-cross streamlets. The creek was headed northwest and about a quarter of a mile beyond the grove, it joined a larger stream which swirled treacherously. Men and mules had already drowned trying to ford its deceptive waters.

These streams were Cherry Creek and the Platte River. Their banks formed the setting for the violent beginnings of Denver, beginnings that were like a melodrama except that right did not triumph. That melodrama stamped the town with a special character which has been tamed somewhat, yet has never changed. She still loves a smart business deal, and she's famed for her feuds.

But to go back—

It was the 17th of November in 1858 when a lone man, splitting "shooks," or slats, for roofing in the cottonwood grove on the northeast side of Cherry Creek, was astounded to see a group of nine strange men suddenly appear. They began to drive stakes and Charles Nichols stopped splitting shooks.

"You can't jump this townsite! It's been surveyed and staked out for over a month. We have a prior right. This cabin proves it."

"Old Charley" spoke up sharply, his voice hallooing out in the Indian summer sunshine. He planted his feet with a defiant stance on the prairie bank where the city of Denver was to grow.

The spot was just about at the approach of today's Blake Street bridge as it starts across the creek to the foot of the Fourteenth Street viaduct, sometimes called Speer viaduct (see map on page 26). Now, it gives no idea of having been once in a remote corner of Kansas Territory. The cabin that Charlie was boasting of, was not much to see—built of rude cottonwood logs with an unfinished slat roof. Yet it represented the

WHERE CHERRY CREEK JOINS THE PLATTE

In the autumn of 1858, after William Green Russell found gold close by, the little settlement of Auraria, now West Denver, sprang up as a row of log cabins. On the south side of Cherry Creek where the Indians liked to camp, Denver City was soon platted. Shown is Colorado's first successful commercial enterprise, the ferry across the Platte, as it busily aided a line of covered wagons on their way to 'them thar hills.'

vision that seven men who had crossed the plains in September from Lawrence, Kansas, saw for the future of the new gold discoveries.

"You can't hold an entire townsite alone," General William Larimer, Jr., replied as he strode forward from the group of strangers.

His particular company was later to become known to history as "the Leavenworth Party" because the starting point for their trip to investigate the rumors of fresh gold fields was Leavenworth, Kansas. They had arrived the night before at the little settlement of Auraria with a four-yoke ox team hitched to a wagon and saddle ponies enough for all.

Auraria was on the southwest side of Cherry Creek. It consisted of five or six crude log cabins, just completed, with a few more in the process of being built, and an assortment of tents and covered wagons that served as temporary living quarters.

"I'm not alone," Old Charley answered. "We have a company—the St. Charles Town Association. We drew up our constitution the last of

September and William Hartley did the surveying in October. He ran the lines for a few streets and our secretary, Dickson, drove that stake over there claiming a square mile."

"A square mile?"

"You can read for yourself the penciling on it. Now he and our president—he's Adnah French—have gone back to Kansas. They'll get a bill before the legislature to incorporate our town. It's named 'St. Charles'."

The Larimer group moved over to the grove, belligerently scuffing their boots in the dust of the prairie land they claimed was theirs.

"There ain't a stake here," they declared. And they were right. Both the tall penciled sapling and the auxiliary stakes were gone—perhaps judiciously spirited away the night before by one of their own members.

Charley Nichols stared incredulously and then swore.

"I'll go get the squaw men, John Smith and William McGaa. We got our title through them and their Indian relatives."

"So did we—our title gives us *all* the land on this side of the Creek—not just a square mile."

Charley rushed off over the creek bed to find the Indian traders who had double-crossed him. Also to get further corroboration from the responsible men of the Auraria City Town Company. Dr. Levi Russell, secretary of Auraria, knew the whole situation although, actually, no one had a right to the land. It was Indian Territory. The shrewd trader Smith and the worthless McGaa, destined to die some years later in the Denver jail as a derelict drunk, had misrepresented their ability to give title. All three town companies—the Auraria, the St. Charles and the Denver—were just squatters.

The newcomers, the Leavenworth Party, had been sold the same fraud as the other two but they included three friends of James W. Denver, then governor of Kansas Territory. Before setting off across the plains in the direction of the gold fields, these three men entreated Denver to appoint them probate judge, county supervisor, and sheriff of Arapahoe County; and the governor, misled by the ballooning reports of mining activities on the South Platte, had given an official stamp to their real estate junket. In return, the group decided to give the new town the governor's name— Denver City.

Charles Nichols pled his cause all morning to the traders and Aurarians, but no one cared. Everyone said Auraria was to be the only important town, anyway. Samuel Curtis, who had helped him build the landmark cabin in return for shares in the St. Charles Company, did substantiate his story—but he was the only man who would. Curtis (after whom Curtis Street is named) stated the truth firmly to the newcomers but they paid no attention. General Larimer was already settling his belongings in Nichols' cabin. The promoter had summarily appropriated

PROTECTION FROM THE INDIANS IN THE '60s

During the long dangerous haul across the plains, the circle formation was used each night by muleteers when they pulled up their covered wagons to camp. Their valuable freight was thus turned into a fortress and helped insure its reaching the destination of Denver. The fifteen-unit train shown on Market Street between 15th and 16th (then Holladay between F and G) provided six mules and a driver for each wagon pulled.

it while making plans to build a cabin of his own and to organize his Denver Company. He had already announced a meeting to be held that night in McGaa's Auraria cabin and no one of the Leavenworth Party would listen to either Curtis or Nichols.

That evening, Samuel Curtis was indignantly ejected from the Auraria Town Company for having allied himself with Old Charley Nichols (who was thirty-six which was considered venerable in the young pioneer settlement) and the beginnings of a feud between Auraria and Denver were laid.

Charley knocked at the McGaa cabin to protest once more against the injustice of the Larimer "steal."

The Denver City promoters greeted him with a peremptory: "Now, you get out of here—and stay out—or the next time you try to make trouble, we'll use a rope and noose on you."

Old Charley slunk back to his tent and they went on with their meeting. Five days later, on November 22, forty-one members adopted a constitution, elected officers and arranged for Samuel Curtis and J. S. Lowry to survey, plat and stake three hundred and twenty acres. As a sop to the St. Charles men, they cut in Old Charley and his six departed associates as shareholders of the Denver City Company and hastily dispatched E. W. Wynkoop back to Kansas to obtain a charter of incorporation for the new town.

The ironic denouement came in February, 1859, when the legislature granted a charter to the St. Charles men and not to the Denver group. But when the St. Charles incorporators returned in the spring, they were unable to oust the Denverites. By then the usurpers had built some forty cabins, fanning out from the first four built at each corner of Fifteenth and Larimer Streets. Possession proved to be ten-tenths of the law.

So Denver was founded on a jumped claim. Underlying this shady theatrical performance was a repeating historical pattern—that of man's lust for gold and of man's different ways for obtaining it. First, there were the brave explorers who wanted to dig it out of the ground; then the traders who liked to finagle for it, and finally the promoters who expected to sell real estate. Each played a part at the birth of the Mile-High City. But it was gold that brought all three to the junction of Cherry Creek with the Platte.

The gold seekers had arrived the preceding June, led by William Green Russell, a Georgian miner who was discouraged with the lessening deposits in his home state. Russell organized a company of over a hundred men, including his two brothers, to journey to what is now Colorado by following up the Arkansas River. They passed the present site of Pueblo and moved northward to camp beside the waters of the Platte in the vicinity of present Denver. Most of them became discouraged when they found only a backbreaking existence in the wilderness and no gold, and straggled back across the plains. The little band of thirteen who remained finally found the gold they sought. Their discovery was about where Englewood is now, just south of the city limits. It wasn't a lot of gold—about enough for each man to pan ten dollars' worth a day—but it was enough to start a lot of rumors.

America was restless in those days. The first gold rush in 1849 to California had accustomed people to looking at far horizons. When Horace Greeley, influential editor of the New York *Tribune,* wrote an 1850 editorial, entitled "Go West, Young Man, Go West," he was not coining a phrase but expressing the thinking of the people. This feeling continued to prevail all during the '50s, and when the news broke of another gold supply in the region of Pikes Peak, they set out.

Would-be miners began converging from all directions, not in great numbers at first, but steadily. Russell knew that the source of the gold lay somewhere in the mountains. So he left some of the men working their small placer, called Montana Diggings, and, with the rest, spent the summer resolutely tramping the hills. But to no avail.

When he got back to camp and conferred with his brothers and the entire company, they decided that what was needed was more men and supplies. Green and Oliver Russell were selected to return to the "States" while Levi and a few others would remain to winter on the Platte. Since the gold deposits at Montana Diggings had largely petered out, they decided to move their camp a few miles downstream to the junction with Cherry Creek, where there were shade trees.

This spot was a famous camping ground for Indians and traders and such notable explorers as Fremont and Long also had stopped here. The men found tents pitched in the grove, those of William McGaa and John Simpson Smith. These two squaw men offered to give a deed to the land, saying that it really belonged to their Indian wives. An agreement was drawn up and, in no time at all, a new town was born, named after the Russells' home in Georgia, Auraria.

The first cabin built was a double one, crudely constructed to house Green Russell and William McGaa. After this residence was finished, thus establishing Russell's rights, the Georgian left for the East, leading those of the party who planned to return in the spring. The men who remained, platted their town and began to fell trees for other cabins. Before winter set in, they planned to have a real "city."

Today, this section is a desolate part of west Denver, mostly dump-strewn vacant lots and railroad yards, down underneath the Fourteenth Street viaduct in the general vicinity of Twelfth and Wewatta Streets. But in 1858 the spot was very pretty, a suitable setting for beginning one's castle in El Dorado and dreaming large dreams, with a view across the foothills to the mysterious Shining Mountains.

The Aurarians were an industrious lot and welcomed each set of newcomers whole-heartedly until they found that some were plotting to set up a rival town company. That made them angry. But even though the second town did materialize, their Auraria was twice as important. It was only after the feud was healed in 1860 by the far-seeing elements in both towns that Denver City forged ahead.

From the very first, colorful characters abounded in the new settlement. "Uncle Dick" Wootton (Richings L.) arrived in Auraria on Christmas morning, bringing two wagons full of merchandise from New Mexico. He set up his tents and began a thriving business. Part of his goods comprised two barrels of raw whiskey, known as Taos Lightning. He knocked in the head of one of these barrels, laid out a supply of tin cups, and invited the populace to dip in.

All Auraria soon called and the news spread across to Denver City like racing tumbleweeds. The flowing contents of that barrel acted as a

AN A. E. MATHEWS PRINT OF 1866 DENVER

A British artist arrived in Denver in the autumn of 1865 and spent the next nine years sketching Western scenes for lithographs. He died near Estes Park at the age of forty-three, and his work has since become a collector's item because of its sensitivity and fidelity. This view portrays 15th Street, as it stretched away toward Capitol Hill, with ox-drawn wagons, mule-drawn carts and Estabrook's prancing black team.

dove of peace. It submerged the last vestige of rancorous rivalry between the two "cities"; and also a number of worthy citizens.

By spring, the newcomers had turned into a swarm and by summer, into a melee. In the middle of June, Auraria had two hundred and fifty cabins and Denver City, slightly more than half that many. But most of these were vacant. Everyone was away in the hills looking for gold. The "Pikes Peak or Bust" rush was at its height.

Denver was just a point of departure. People were always leaving it. The miners left to surge into the mountains; the traders left to seek supplies or equipment in the East, and the tenderfeet left to return home, there to curse it loudly. Denver was just a way station.

But curiously enough, without much reason for its existence, it continued to grow. Despite its being only a way station, the settlement developed a tough independent quality that began to be known. As this special flavor became more established, the town attracted men of spectacular fiber.

A few of these men were fine, like William Gilpin, Colorado's first territorial governor who had been an explorer and had written a book, "The Central Gold Region." Shrewd, civic-minded John Evans, the second territorial governor, who already had founded Northwestern University

THE WINDSOR HOTEL RULED THE '80s

Except for the porte-cocheres, now gone, the Windsor is much the same as when it was opened in June, 1880, and became the social center of Colorado. Built by an English company, the building flew the American flag on its main tower and the Windsor and English flags from two lesser towers. Largest shareholder was H. A. W. Tabor, richest man in Colorado, who lived there at various times and died there, destitute.

and for whom Evanston, Illinois, was named, was another of this group. In Colorado, he founded Denver University and the dominant peak of the Front Range was called Evans.

Still another was intrepid William N. Byers who hauled a press across the prairie and started *The Rocky Mountain News* in the second floor of Uncle Dick Wootton's log cabin store, which served as Denver's first business building. Byers was forced to defend his editorial opinions with gunfire and to outwit kidnappers as well; but he lived to a serene old age. David Moffat, who began as a clerk in a bookstore and built a banking and investment fortune, only to squander every penny in trying to realize his dream of a transcontinental railroad through Colorado, was one more outstanding early-comer.

Sometimes these first arrivals were delightfully, or boldly, eccentric—like the Frenchman, Count Henri Murat, who claimed to be a nephew of Bonaparte's King of Naples and who shaved men's beards for the sum of one dollar, a sum he referred to as "paltry." Horace Greeley who arrived in June on an early stagecoach to write up John Gregory's discovery of lode gold in the gulch that cradled Central City, was one of his customers. The noted editor referred to the "paltry" price with heavy sarcasm.

Oliver J. Goldrick drove an ox-drawn covered wagon into town, attired for his bull-whacking job in a frock coat, silk hat, white cravat and lemon-colored gloves, and proceeded to address the populace in faultless Latin. He became the town's first teacher and school principal. Then there was that military fanatic, Major John M. Chivington, who acted the hero of the battle of Glorieta Pass in 1862 and metamorphosed into the villain of the Sand Creek Massacre in 1864, when he slaughtered defenseless squaws and their papooses.

But most of the first citizens were just plain bad. They included gamblers like tall, twenty-two-year-old Ed Chase who outlasted all comers and nearly every wave of reform. He perched on a high stool, a shotgun in the crook of his arm; but he never had to use it. The steel in his eyes was enough. And Ed Chase, despite a series of sensational amours and successive wives, was a respectable citizen alongside most of his associates.

The most notorious resident was Charley Harrison, gambler and proprietor of the Criterion Saloon, which was the hangout of a mob of cut-throats. Harrison was outwardly a charming Southerner; but he committed one murder after another, and through his henchmen, terrorized the new community with murders and other violences. A Vigilante Committee was powerless. When finally he was brought to trial for one of his murders, the proceedings turned out to be nothing but a two-day farce. The twelve good men and true had already been softened up with $5,000 distributed by Ada Lamont, a woman of the streets, and the jury could not agree. The prisoner was released. So extraordinary was Harrison's life story that in recent years R. D. Andrews has incorporated it in a novel, "Great Day in the Morning."

Ada Lamont, Harrison's friend, who found the reckless atmosphere of Denver to her liking, was another typical character of the times. Despite being arrested twice in 1866, during one of Denver's waves of reform, she prospered and used her profits to become a madam. For a while she operated a house in Georgetown, but in the early '70s moved back to Denver where her bordello was the scene of a sordid murder, only one of many committed along "The Line." By then, she was elegantly calling herself Mme. La Monte.

As more wealth was produced in the mountains, the bad 'uns included desperadoes like the Reynolds Gang. They stole horses and held up stagecoaches that were returning from the mines with gold dust and retorts bound for the mint. When caught in 1864, Jim Reynolds and most of the gang were later deliberately lined up and shot. But John Reynolds escaped to New Mexico and some years later, desperately wounded from another robbery, he passed on to a friend a penciled map. The sketch showed where the gang had buried some stolen Colorado treasure in Elk Creek, about forty miles from Denver. Campers are still looking for it.

A strange assortment—these early Denver citizens; yet taken all together they made the town an extraordinary settlement, where, according to Horace Greeley, there were "more brawls, more pistol shots with criminal intent . . . than in any community with equal numbers on earth" and where, in the words of Wootton, murders were "almost every day occurrences." Uncle Dick went on to say that "stealing was the only occupation of a considerable portion of the population, who would take anything from a pet calf, or a counterfeit gold dollar, up to a saw mill."

But the better citizens persevered, fighting violence with lynchings, and dodging Indians on the warpath. In their several and sometimes peculiar ways, these Denver citizens gave their town a loyalty that caused it to surge out ahead. Within a few years, Denver dominated the whole of a new territory created in 1861, named Colorado, and achieved the status both of capital and principal city. As the Indians were pushed back, its influence was felt throughout all of the Rocky Mountain West.

Its first spectacular triumph came in 1862 when the Civil War was gripping the nation. The Southerners had conceived a brilliant tactical move, namely to send a force from Texas up the valley of the Rio Grande, that would capture New Mexico and Colorado, shutting off the North's gold supply from California and from the new mines near Denver. If this were successful, the Confederates would then march east through Kansas and surprise Grant in the rear.

The Texans were amazingly successful and everything was going according to plan. The Rio Grande valley, Albuquerque and Santa Fe fell to them on schedule and the Southerners were headed north. Then the Coloradans made a forced march from Denver, covering, at the last, a tramp of ninety-two miles in thirty-six hours. Heroically they met the enemy at Apache Canyon, New Mexico, in a fierce and apparently losing battle but, through a clever circling maneuver by Chivington and his men at Glorieta Pass, the Confederates' supply train was cut off. The battle was won, and the Texans were forced back to El Paso. The indomitable spirit of Denver had preserved the North's cause and the battle was proudly called "the Gettysburg of the West."

Denver was presented with other prickly problems—a disastrous fire in 1863, and an obliterating flood in 1864 and, after the Civil War was over, it was faced with an economic threat worse than any military

BABY DOE TABOR AND HER WEDDING DRESS

The Tabor exhibit in the Colorado State Museum at 14th and Sherman Streets draws more tourists than any other spot. This perennial popularity proves that no other Colorado legend has such appeal. Baby Doe's life is told in "Silver Queen;" in the case are her $7,000 bridal gown and a photograph of her diamond necklace, once Queen Isabella's.

crisis. She had always thought of her mountains as an asset but now they portended death. Although the view from the State Capitol is magnificent, the casual observer, as he oh's and ah's, seldom analyzes what he sees. The mountains are beautiful, yes, but they are also a barrier. In the whole of the United States there are only sixty-seven peaks over fourteen thousand feet; yet fifty-two of them rear up in the western half of Colorado. Not a very good location for a town that wished to be a way station when a transcontinental route was impossible!

Even in an era of flagrant land grabs and get-rich subsidies, no railroad was willing to attempt to cross the continent by way of these insurmountable fifty-two peaks. The Santa Fe went south through New Mexico and the Union Pacific built north through Wyoming. Denver was left shunned and isolated. Property values fell and the town appeared

BROWN PALACE

No hotel in America has a more bizarre history than Denver's best. Built in 1892, it was named for the man who donated land to build the Capitol — Henry C. Brown. Often the scene of strange goings-on, from prize bulls in the lobby to murders in the bar, it was once bought by W. C. Stratton, the "Midas of the Rockies," so that he could prevent creditors from ejecting the owner, his old friend, H. C. Brown.

to be doomed. Scores of families left and moved up to Cheyenne which, they believed, would be the coming metropolis.

But the less than four thousand citizens of Denver, although dismayed, did not despair. Again they valiantly met the emergency. They organized a Board of Trade to create their own railroad and, in one week in the autumn of 1867, raised $280,000 (which was later augmented to $640,000 by Arapahoe County bonds since Denver was the county seat). With this money they organized the Denver Pacific Railroad and started grading a roadbed for a spur to meet the main line of the Union Pacific in Cheyenne. The road was completed in June, 1870. With jubilant ceremony and oratory, the last spike was driven—a solid silver one from the mines at Georgetown to symbolize that once more Denver had conquered.

She really had. The day the spike was driven, her population numbered 4,759, a total that was less than the population of the Central City gulch towns. But with the advent of her railroad, soon followed by the Kansas Pacific coming straight west across the prairie, the days of caroming stagecoaches, of breathless riders for the pony express and Indians on the warpath, were over. In the next decade her population soared to 35,629 and she began to preen herself as the Queen City of the Plains.

Although she was growing very rapidly and her streets were no longer lined by log cabins and wooden structures with false fronts, her character remained the same. The business buildings might be turning into brick structures, but the sidewalks were still board and the water ran along the gutters in open ditches. The surface might be more presentable but if it were scratched, the blatant rawness of the frontier showed through. In 1872, when Dr. Frederick J. Bancroft, the city physician, made his report to the council, he used a large portion of his message to inveigh against the 'evils and iniquities' of the houses of ill fame, and to demand stricter laws. Bancroft had been a doctor in the community for six years and it was his verdict that "probably every third man who reaches the age of twenty-five, has acquired in these places constitutional syphillis." ·

But the good doctor's plea was in vain. The local authorities ignored him except to make a superficial gesture, from time to time, which consisted mostly in paying a personal call on Byers so that the *News* would run an item to the effect that the "soiled doves" were leaving Denver for a more healthy clime and "the public here are rejoiced." This was mere pretense and the red-light district continued to flourish scandalously.

Its locale was along the street originally known as McGaa, named in honor of the family whose baby son, William Denver McGaa, was the first child born in Denver—in a wigwam at Fourteenth and Lawrence. The street's name was later changed to Holladay to compliment Ben Holloday, operator of the overland stagecoach lines. But in the hurry and excitement of frontier life, it was spelled wrong!

During the '70s and '80s, "The Row" consisted of three city blocks, lined with cribs and parlor houses on both sides of the street. This section developed such a bad name for its wildness and wickedness that successful madams from the mining camps and dressy madams from the East began moving in to open up and add to the notoriety. The most sensational arrivals were probably pretty, blonde Mattie Silks, who always had a canny eye for business and who came down from Georgetown in 1876, and beautiful, brown-haired Jennie Rogers, who swept into town in 1880 from Pittsburgh and bought her first Holladay street house from Mattie Silks, plunking out $4,600 with her usual dash.

The career of this bawdy street was long-lived and apparently unassailable. It ran wide open (although once again under a new name, Market) until 1915 when at long last the respectable forces of the community made themselves felt. But for half a century, the attitude of the town was so patent that in August, 1880, both the *Republican* and the *Rocky Mountain News* reported that the city council had failed to transact

any business on the 19th because a quorum was not present. They pointed out that the absentees preferred to attend "the opening of a new and fashionable den of prostitution on Holladay St." The *News* added, "A mob may take that council in hand yet." But no such thing ever occurred.

The town was also still a way station. Boomers were always rushing off to a new strike and then returning to the town, either flat broke or to blow in their new wealth. In the '70s, Central City, Idaho Springs, Georgetown, South Park and Breckenridge were superseded by the San Juans, Deadwood, Leadville and Aspen as successive spots for hectic rushes. The cry now was for silver more than for gold, and the most dizzying jumps to riches were based on silver-and-lead carbonates rather than on gold pyrites. The most talked-of vault was that of Horace Tabor who in a single year ran a seventeen-dollar grub stake of groceries, that he gave to two prospectors, into a twenty-million-dollar company.

The stay-at-home citizens of Denver profited directly and indirectly by the good fortune that was enveloping the state. They sometimes made direct investments in the mining activities that absorbed the mountain areas, and, in any case, it was their business to supply the necessary merchandise and equipment to keep the mining towns going. Also, there was the cattle industry on the plains to the east, equally prosperous; and along the Platte and Arkansas valleys, despite two years of grasshopper plagues, agricultural communities were beginning to grow. In the center was Denver, so located as to partake in the honey of each money-making venture that blossomed.

The more sober civic minds turned their attention to founding schools, colleges, hospitals, to organizing legislation and writing a constitution preparatory to obtaining statehood. On the Fourth of July in 1876, the adoption of the constitution was celebrated with a joyous parade, a patriotic program and a picnic in the cottonwood grove on the banks of the Platte. Floats were elaborate and colorful; the last one to pass carried thirty-seven girls, each representing a state of the Union, while the thirty-eighth, Miss Colorado, had the place of honor. She was a native-born girl chosen for her prettiness. Seventy-five years later in 1951, as Mrs. Mary Butler Brown, she was still alive to take part in several commemorative celebrations, especially on August 1, Colorado Day, the date President Grant created the state.

During the '70s, Denverites also turned their attention to railroad building and this decade saw the beginnings of narrow gauge track so laid that it became an engineering and scenic wonder to the whole world. The little steel rails twisted snakelike through tortuous canyons and surmounted ten- and eleven-thousand-foot passes. These feats only emphasized anew the toughness of the small town on the edge of the plains. Obstacles were like mustangs to bronco-busting cowboys—something to saddle and break.

The '80s were even more bountiful than expected. The long burro and mule pack-trains, trudging their perilous way along stony mountain trails, began to return with treasure. As people made money in the mountains, some families returned East, but most chose Denver as a permanent residence. Nathaniel P. Hill, who made a fortune treating ores in Blackhawk from 1869 to 1878, decided to move his smelter down to Argo, just outside Denver, and his action started a migration.

Each new family from the mining towns began breaking ground for a mansion. Generally, they chose a pretentious style built of large sandstone blocks, replete with turrets, bays, and leaded windows, surrounded by heavy copings with either white marble lions at the entrance or cast-iron deer on the lawn. The houses were as fancified and as protuberant as the ladies' bustles. The older citizens gave up their more modest frame or brick houses, in what is now the downtown section, and moved to Capitol Hill to compete with the new millionaires from Central City and Leadville. Fashion dictated a scale of living as lavish as the language in the latest journalistic innovation—the society column.

Downtown Denver began to change materially. The person who made the greatest single dent in its new facade was Tabor with his fortune from Leadville silver mines. At the opening of the '80s he bought the Henry C. Brown house, on almost a block of ground, running between Broadway and Lincoln Streets at Seventeenth Avenue (this land is now occupied by the Sears-Roebuck parking lot and the Blue Parrot Inn). Then he erected the Tabor Block, helped to complete the Windsor Hotel, built the Tabor Grand Opera House and sold land worth $90,000 for $65,000 to the United States government for a post office site at Sixteenth and Arapahoe Streets, on which was soon built a dignified structure (now a recruiting station).

These buildings were of a magnificence new to the frontier town. The Tabor Block (now the Nassau Building) on the northeast corner of Sixteenth and Larimer Streets cost $200,000 and was of stone quarried in Ohio. In 1880, when the Windsor was opened at Eighteenth and Larimer, it was the last word in elegance. The elite drank at a sixty-foot mahogany bar, danced in a ballroom with elaborate crystal chandeliers and floor of parquetry, and walked through a lobby furnished in thick red carpet and diamond-dust backed mirrors.

But it was nothing compared to the grandeur of the five-storied Tabor Opera House.

For this, Tabor spared no expense. The building is of red pressed brick trimmed with white stone, now dirtied to a dull grey. The interior of the theatre seated fifteen hundred people on fashionable red plush and was finished in cherry wood, imported from Japan. Unfortunately, although the building stands, the theatre has been completely altered to the needs of a movie house, and its grandiose panelling and plush are gone. The sombre, prophetic curtain, painted by Robert Hopkin of Detroit, and described in every book in which the Tabors appear, is still in the stage-loft. It was lowered a number of times in September, 1951, as an exhibit for the theatre's seventieth anniversary.

A gala opening was held in the Opera House in September 1881, with Emma Abbot singing "Lucia" on the stage and another drama being enacted in the audience. Box A, reserved for the Tabor family, was conspicuous by the absence of Mrs. Tabor. The gossips buzzed and craned their necks, trying to see a heavily-veiled, beautiful little blonde, seated toward the rear, who was known as "that infamous Baby Doe."

All through the '80s Denver continued to build and expand. In general, the direction was east, toward the plains, although there was a brief vogue for the Highlands, now north Denver. A number of elaborate houses still anachronistically bear testimony to this period. The elite brownstone Denver Club at Seventeenth and Glenarm Streets, character-istic of the architecture in favor, was built during this decade and became known, because of the immoral gaiety of some of its members, as "the home for fallen men." This sobriquet no doubt carried the acrimony of those who had been snobbishly excluded.

Such was the success of Denver during this period that its population tripled, rising from 35,629 to 106,713. But its main business was still

ELITCH'S THEATER BEGAN IN THE GAY '90s

Denver has the oldest summer stock theater in the U.S.A. It began in 1891 as an added feature of Elitch's Gardens and Amusement Park. Shown is the famous 1928 cast. C. Henry Gordon, Isobel Elsom and Fredric March are in the chariot; Francis Goodrich, Doan Borys, Jassimine Newcomb, standing; Jay Fassett, Edna James Chappell, Sylvia Sidney, Albert Hackett, Francis Compton and Frank McDonald, mounted.

as a supply depot and merchandise mart for the activities that most interested its citizens—the mines in the mountains. It was still, in a very real sense, a way station.

The '90s dawned rosy and clear and promised more of the same. The new bonanza camp of Creede was discovered and, while its roaring life was of short duration, it has achieved immortality in Cy Warman's lines, "Here the meek and mild-eyed burros on mineral mountains feed. It's day all day in the daytime and there is no night in Creede." Denver financiers who had invested heavily in these new silver mines were delightedly licking their chops at the soaring profits.

At home, these prosperous investors were still erecting buildings. Frank C. Young, who had made a tidy pile in Central City, built the exquisite Broadway Theatre. Its gilt boxes resemble miniature mosques and are at each side of an Oriental scene, "A Glimpse of India," painted on the stage curtain. These dainty boxes were filled to capacity on its opening night in August, 1890, when a society crowd, swathed in glistening satins, gathered to hear "Carmen." The famed Brown Palace Hotel and the imposing Equitable Building, at Seventeenth and Stout Streets, opened their doors in August, 1892, with all the fanfare that the town could muster.

But the most grandiloquent gesture accompanied the laying of the cornerstone for the State Capitol, a building of Corinthian architecture designed with a ground plan in the form of a Greek cross. Solid grey granite, quarried near Gunnison, Colorado, was chosen for the walls and the vaulting dome was later covered with two hundred ounces of genuine gold-leaf, bringing the final cost of the building, completed in 1908, to $3,000,000. Speeches were delivered, a band played and a Masonic choir of one thousand voices sang the national anthem.

Then, abruptly, in 1893 prosperity and enthusiasm came to a dead stop. Since the price of silver was largely dependent on the practice of bi-metallism for backing paper money, for several years the hand-writing on the wall had been discernible to a few. President Grover Cleveland was a man committed irrevocably to Wall Street and its insistence on a gold standard. When he returned to office, his first move was to suggest the repeal of the Sherman Silver Purchasing Act. His stand intensified a dropping market. The price of silver went steadily down until, in one four-day period of June, it catapulted twenty-one cents to a paltry sixty-two cents an ounce. Mines and smelters started to shut down, unable to operate at a profit.

The blow fell in mid-July when panic seized the people. They swarmed the streets and stormed the banks. Within three days ten Denver banks failed. Although the crisis was strangling the whole nation and spreading throughout the world, no state was affected as much as Colorado and no city to compare with Denver. In the face of this panic, in August Cleveland called a special session of Congress. Senators Henry M. Teller and Edward O. Wolcott from Denver fought hour after hour through the sticky humid heat of a Washington summer, but failed to sway the Congress. The nation declared for gold alone and Colorado lost her only good silver customer—the government.

Both senators' gloom was intense. They were personally involved in the disaster as well as politically—each had begun his career in the mountains. Teller had first hung out his law shingle in Central City in 1861, and Wolcott, in Georgetown in 1871. They had built up their large legal practises, both there and in Denver, on a knowledge of mining and railroad law. In return, both attorneys had often accepted payment of fees in mining or narrow gauge railway stock—a practise that had made Teller well-to-do, and Wolcott enormously wealthy. In fact, it was this same

WAPITI ELK

The Denver Museum of Natural History is considered the third finest in the United States, and unrivalled in exhibits of indigenous plants and animals. The cases show animals in their native habitat; this one near Mount Evans.

maligned silver, dug from the Little Annie mine at Aspen and the Last Chance at Creede, that had recently made it possible for the junior senator to complete his country show place, "Wolhurst." The return of the two men to Denver was as mournful as a funeral march.

The state and its capital were submerged by depression. Everywhere miners were out of work and descended on Denver for relief. There was none in town—businesses were failing, mortgages were being foreclosed and real estate values were hitting new lows. Hunger and idleness hung like a pall and thousands of unemployed soon produced robberies, violence and murders. For over a year Denver was really down.

In this atmosphere of hopelessness and desperation, her character as a way station still persisted. Some of the unemployed wanted to join "Coxey's Army" which was marching across the nation to petition for relief at the national capital. They built shallow boats and tried to sail down the Platte, but the river's erratic currents and sand-bars proved too formidable. The attempt was a failure.

Those joiners of Coxey's Army who succeeded in leaving town, stole rides on the railroad. But Denver did not notice either their departure or their failure to pay for a ticket—she was too preoccupied with her own problems. She was thirty-five years old and had spent her whole life as a way station—a successful way station—until now, when she was flat and busted.

What should Denver do?

*   *   *

MILE

HIGH

CITY

Denver's fine location is seen in this dramatic air view of the business section. The highest snow peak is Mt. Evans. The most gashed foothill mountain is Morrison, seat of the Red Rocks Amphitheatre. The streets run true to the points of the compass outside the oldest part, where they cut diagonally.

City Hall

Greek Theatre
The Capitol

Catholic Cathedral

Colfax Viaduct
Public Service Bldg.
Continental Oil Bldg.
Daniels and Fisher Tower
Post Office
The Windsor
Federal Bldg.

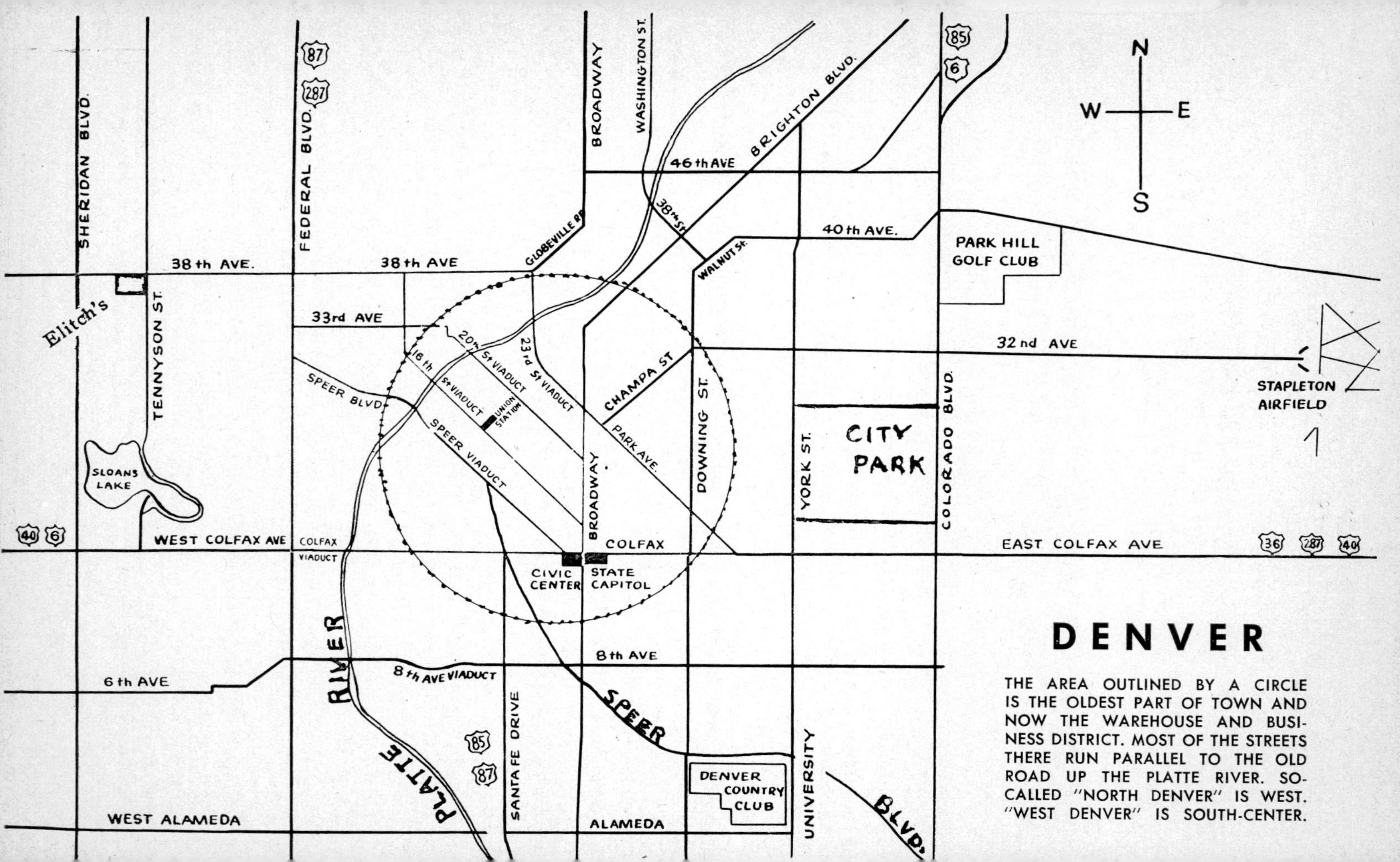
N
W
E
S
SHERIDAN BLVD.
FEDERAL BLVD.
87
287
BROADWAY
WASHINGTON ST.
BRIGHTON BLVD.
85
6
46th AVE
38th St.
40th AVE.
PARK HILL GOLF CLUB
38th AVE.
38th AVE
GLOBEVILLE RD
WALNUT St.
Elitch's
TENNYSON ST.
33rd AVE
32 nd AVE
20th St VIADUCT
16th St VIADUCT
23rd St VIADUCT
CHAMPA ST
PARK AVE.
DOWNING ST.
YORK ST.
COLORADO BLVD.
STAPLETON AIRFIELD
SPEER BLVD
SPEER VIADUCT
UNION STATION
BROADWAY
CITY PARK
SLOANS LAKE
40
6
WEST COLFAX AVE
COLFAX VIADUCT
COLFAX
COLFAX
EAST COLFAX AVE
36
287
40
CIVIC CENTER
STATE CAPITOL
DENVER
8th AVE
6 th AVE
8th AVE VIADUCT
RIVER
PLATTE
85
87
SANTA FE DRIVE
SPEER
DENVER COUNTRY CLUB
UNIVERSITY
BLVD.
WEST ALAMEDA
ALAMEDA
THE AREA OUTLINED BY A CIRCLE
IS THE OLDEST PART OF TOWN AND
NOW THE WAREHOUSE AND BUSI-
NESS DISTRICT. MOST OF THE STREETS
THERE RUN PARALLEL TO THE OLD
ROAD UP THE PLATTE RIVER. SO-
CALLED "NORTH DENVER" IS WEST.
"WEST DENVER" IS SOUTH-CENTER.

TOURIST TOWN

Prostrate from the Silver Panic, Denver suffered. Her former pluck was struggling to assert itself, but the going was as hard as dynamiting through granite. Then, astonishingly, she was saved by luck—the fabulous luck of another gold strike! Gold had made Denver; now gold saved her.

This time, the gold poured in from Cripple Creek, a new camp back of Pikes Peak, where the discovery was made by a hopeful, untutored cowboy working for the Bennett and Myers ranch. Bob Womack made a habit of picking up stray rocks. Despite thirty-odd years of ceaseless searching in every gulch and cranny of Colorado by seasoned prospectors, none had ever suspected the grassy meadow where Womack took his sample. But the cowboy's fluke uncovered the biggest bonanza of the state's history and the richest gold camp in the United States.

In 1894, the camp produced two million dollars in gold and in the next year trebled this sum. The annual amount climbed to seven, to ten, to thirteen, and finally to eighteen million dollars by 1900. During the next ten years after that, the district's average production annually was $15,000,000. No one had ever seen anything like it and Denver immediately profited.

A fresh wave of millionaires descended; among them, Horace Bennett and Verner Z. Reed. The most fantastic overnight moneybags was W. S. Stratton, "Midas of the Rockies" as he is called by his biographer, Frank Waters. Stratton lived in Colorado Springs but he made frequent trips to Denver to carouse, to shop for his current light-of-love, or to make investments, especially in Denver real estate.

According to an apocryphal story, it was on one of these trips that he bought the Brown Palace Hotel in order to fire a night clerk who displeased him. It seems to be true that he was once enraged when rebuked for some episode involving drink, noise, or a girl in his rooms. But he did not buy the Brown Palace until his old friend, Henry C. Brown, the formerly wealthy builder and owner of the hotel, who had been caught short by the Silver Panic, was about to be ejected from his suite by demanding creditors. Stratton bought the mortgage in order to save this very elderly gentleman, hard pressed and cornered, whose case appealed to his pity.

Stratton's philanthropic feeling was proverbial. Only he, of all Colorado, came to Tabor's assistance when the crash of '93 ruined the one-time Silver King and completely swept away the state's most colossal fortune. Stratton loaned Tabor $15,000 and later tore up the note. Perhaps the most characteristic story of Stratton's generosity occurred shortly after his Independence Mine at Cripple Creek began pouring forth gold. The new millionaire saw a laundry woman, her back bent and her feet dragging, while she tried to carry home a large bundle of laundry. He promptly ordered a bicycle, equipped with a handle-bar basket, for every laundry woman in Colorado Springs.

The Cripple Creek gold rolled in simultaneously with a bumper farm crop following several years of drought. The light-hearted gaiety that accompanied the new wealth from both mountains and plains completely rejuvenated Denver. The city began to be thankful, and as her thankfulness mounted, she wanted to show her gratitude publicly.

The outcome of this feeling was the "Festival of Mountain and Plain." It ran for four days in October, 1895, and was repeated annually, sometimes running as long as a week, through the rest of the century. It was revived twice thereafter, in 1901 and in 1912; and the possibility of holding another one is suggested every now and then. But its huge success probably was dependent on the lavish spirit of the Golden Nineties.

Every day there was a parade. The last one took place at eight o'clock at night, a "Grand Allegorical parade by the Slaves of the Silver Serpent; a gorgeous pageant that will rival the ideal Mardi Gras," in the words of the Official Program. In truth, some of the floats had been shipped from New Orleans and were as copiously decorated as any in the world. The leading float bore an enormous shining Silver Serpent, symbol of Colorado's power and nemesis.

The King of the Slaves of the Silver Serpent followed next. Queen Thalia, a young woman chosen for her beauty, and a bevy of ladies-in-waiting, who ruled over the whole Festival, had the place of honor in the parade. The Queen's court costume was of white and yellow satin, the carnival colors; the sleeves were ornamented in pearls and the skirt had a train five yards long.

An eerie, twisting block-long serpent, that writhed from one side of the street to the other, was made of phosphorescent silver cloth and carried on the heads of hundreds of marchers. The serpent "laid an iridescent radiance upon the city," in the words of an Eastern reporter from *Harpers Weekly,* who was agog at the doings in 1897.

Following the last night parade there was a society ball, presided over by the King and Queen and the Slaves of the Silver Serpent, staged at

MAGNIFICENT VIEW FROM THE CAPITOL

Beyond the civic center, city hall and hospitality center are the snow peaks, Logan, alone to the left; Rosalie, Epaulet, Evans, Spalding, Rogers and Goliath in a group; Bard, Parnassus, Robeson, and Englemann (just opposite Berthoud Pass) in the next, and Cone, Flora, Witter, Eva, Bancroft, and James in the northernmost group. Three heavily timbered mountains are Meridian, Squaw (a snow patch as papoose) and Santa Fe. The five most prominent foothills are Morrison, Lookout (with Buffalo Bill's grave), Centennial Cone, Douglas and Blackhawk.

the Brown Palace Hotel where a new Queen Thalia was chosen for the coming year.

The very first parade of the opening Festival threw a fright into the committee and, very briefly, some whispered that it was an unpropitious omen. The team of horses hitched to the first float, balked in terror at all the strange contraptions. But a new team was substituted and when they proved more philosophical, the line got in motion successfully. Its floats displayed exhibits of Colorado mining, agriculture, horticulture, live stock, manufacturing, civic societies and schools. A hundred thousand people witnessed their passage and stayed for the succeeding events.

That first year, the program included an illuminated trolley musicale, cyclist exhibitions, Pueblo and Ute Indian dances, miners' rock drill contests, cavalry and infantry drills, and band contests. To these were added, in following years, a stagecoach shot at by "twelve good Indians" (who could be trusted not to injure the passengers), a balloon ascension and parachute jump, a mock emergency night call of the Fire Department ("a soul-thrilling dash, lit with a thousand torches," according to the Official Program), a masked ball with dancing in the streets climaxed by

WINTER SIGHT

Stock Show visitors are familiar with the gay lights on Denver's City Hall and the annual specially-built Christmas tree in the Civic Center. This feature is held over to delight stockmen until late in January.

a Grand Prize Cake Walk, fireworks at City Park, a horse show, a street fair, and a rodeo. And each year, the pageantry surrounding Queen Thalia, her attendants and Slaves grew more vivid and complicated.

According to the *Rocky Mountain News,* the second year was attended by a hundred thousand from Denver and fifty thousand tourists. Some of the latter included the "high officials of Ak-Sar-Ben of Omaha getting pointers regarding festival shows." For the third year, the Festival crowds included "thousands from Cripple Creek" (present population 853). By the turn of the century, Denver and its Festival of Mountain and Plain were definitely established as a tourist attraction.

Although this annual festival was abandoned, its success did create a number of customs which have taken firm root in the town and state. Its street fair developed into the annual State Fair at Pueblo, and its horse show and rodeo were the forerunner of the National Western Stock Show, held each January in Denver since 1907. Its offer at the 1901 rodeo of a "Championship Rough Riders' Belt of the World" was the first of its kind. Despite the fact that public rodeos had been taking place throughout the West since the late '80s, and Denver had held its first rodeo in 1887, ten years before the commencement of Cheyenne's "Frontier Days," this was the first attempt to create a champion. It established Denver as a preeminent contest spot for the cowboys.

Other contemporary factors were helping to change Denver's character and to make her less single-tracked in pursuit of ore bodies. After the painful singeing that "Seventeenth Street," Denver's financial district, took in the Silver Panic, venture capital was more and more difficult to obtain for developing mines. The investors were turning to less speculative outlets—to reclamation projects, to experiments with agricultural specialties

SUMMER STARS

The Chamberlin Observatory of Denver University is a popular spot two nights each week when tourists may look at the sparkling firmament without charge. It is at East Warren and Fillmore St., near D.U.

such as Rocky Ford cantaloupe and Pascal celery, to horticultural splendors such as the Colorado carnation, to the incipient sugar beet industry, to real estate development, and to tourist attractions. When the mining camps asked for money, Denver increasingly shrugged an answer that meant "once burned—twice shy."

Except for the Colorado carnations, Denver played no unique part in the "green thumb" experimentation, other than to loan money. But that hardy, fragrant flower, which is now publicized in national magazine color lay-outs, was born within the city limits. In a greenhouse near Berkeley Lake the first attempt was made in 1891 to grow carnations under glass. From that first tender stem has grown an industry that ships Colorado carnations all over the world. The coronation of George VI, in 1937, provided the largest single over-seas order; but, currently, the flowers are sent by plane and train out of Denver in large quantities every day. They have been successfully shipped ever since 1906, when a Colorado Springs florist established the feasibility. Also, it is due to the Colorado carnation that in 1919 a couple of Denver florists first thought of the idea of delivering flowers by telegraph.

Diversification of interests brought to town people who saw Denver as an opportunity, not just as a way station. They planned new projects based within the city limits, not with their eyes on mines in the mountains. The two liveliest and most picturesque of this type were Frederick G. Bonfils and Harry H. Tammen, an odd pair—flamboyant, noisy, belligerent, emotional, but shrewd and avaricious for power. In 1895, they bought an anemic newspaper property, *The Denver Post;* leased a new office on Sixteenth Street opposite the Tabor Theatre, and set out to put the paper, themselves and the town of Denver on the map of the Rocky Mountain West.

Jovial, pudgy Harry Tammen had been in Denver since 1880. He had worked his way up from busboy, through bartender, to owning and operating two enterprises—a curio shop that specialized in colorful mineral specimens and Indian arrowheads, and the publication of a magazine, *The Great Divide,* devoted to western lore.

He used to crack a joke about himself and his way with money. When he was a bartender behind the sixty-foot mahogany grandeur of the Windsor bar, many influential nabobs used to gather there to lean and transact big deals, while convivially "treating." Often drinks were paid for with five-dollar gold pieces.

"I'd pick up those coins," went Tammen's story, "and throw them up to the ceiling. Those that stuck belonged to the management. Those that came down were mine."

Apparently not enough of them had come down, for in 1895 when Tammen heard that the *Post* was for sale, and wanted to buy it, he had neither gold nor silver—only brass. A mutual friend told him of a dashing thirty-four-year-old buccaneer, F. G. Bonfils, who was looking for a new investment and Harry Tammen, then thirty-nine, went to Chicago to meet him. Tammen outlined his idea—

"Newspapers are the coming thing. You've got money and I've got brains. Let's buy it."

Handsome, dapper "F. G." was captivated by the stranger who had no gold "but all the brass in the world," as he later described the meeting, and he agreed to the plan. Together, they bought *The Denver Post* for $12,500, and in November, 1895, announced the new management to a meager six thousand subscribers. It was a staid announcement, in keeping with the type and style the newspaper had been using. But that was the last time the *Post* was ever staid. Denver was in for a jolt.

"We want all Denver to talk about the *Post,*" Bonfils said.

"Make this paper like a vaudeville show," were Tammen's orders. "Play up every sort of stunt. Make the readers cry, laugh, gasp or shudder, but see that they *feel* something."

They began running headlines on the front page in red ink. The startling color and the flashy composition astounded the public. First, people bought the paper out of curiosity. Soon they were buying it because the columns contained more local items than its competitors, and the news was better written. Every extra cent that "Bon and Tam" could lay their hands on went to hire the best newspaper talent available and thus make up deficiencies in their our journalistic knowledge. The combined production was a seven-day wonder.

The vested interests did not like the rampaging new team nor their lambasting editorials, printed under the caption: "So the People May Know." David Moffat, one of the banking and mining powers on Sev-

MUSEUM DIRECTOR'S DELIGHT

Such is the nickname for the Schleier Gallery unit of the Denver Art Museum, located on the south side of the Civic Center. It was transformed from a factory by Burnham Hoyt and has a huge unbroken space which can be rearranged to fit each exhibition with portable walls and cases. Its ceiling is an all-over aluminum grid with four-inch squares, giving perfect indirect lighting and acoustical properties.

enteenth Street, who also owned *The Denver Times,* instigated a boycott of the *Post* by the advertisers.

Denver's answer was soon plain. The town's preference showed up in the circulation figures, which mounted in two years from 6,000 subscribers to 24,599. Soon the advertisers could not afford to ignore the *Post.* If they wanted to reach the great middle class, "The Best Newspaper in the U. S. A." was the only practical medium. The public loved the attacks, the crusades and the stunts and bought the paper to see what Bon and Tam were up to next. Every evening the small home-owner lounged back in his reading chair with a metaphorical "Sic 'em, Fido!" Denver had been born in a feud, and was still partial to a scrap.

As the *Post* prospered, it grew cockier and cockier and took on all comers. It made enemies, but it succeeded. Its financial position grew more solid; for, as Lawrence Martin has shown in his excellently written paper-bound history of the *Post,* "So the People May Know," the partners plowed back all their profits for thirteen years. They were trying to entrench the newspaper as an indisputable leader in the community.

On one count, it did have a profound influence. "The Paper With a Heart and a Soul" made Denver conscious of its economic opportunities as the center of a whole section of the country. It showed that the people

Frederic H. Douglas, for many years curator of Indian art at the Denver Art Museum, has brought the showing of native arts to a new pictorial level, as in this exhibit of a Pueblo Corn Dance. It shows their pottery, weaving, masks, costumes and customs at a glance.

of this region were supported by many diverse occupations, not just one or two. It also made Denver aware of its position as the gateway to a thousand views of breath-taking scenery. Here was a chance to play host to a nation—with both climate and natural beauty as lures to the visitor.

Even more influential in turning the Mile High City into a tourist town was Mayor Robert W. Speer, first elected to that four-year office in 1904. To win the election, he put on a rip-snorting campaign in which he bought up every billboard in town. All the newspapers were opposed to him and this was the only way he had to give the rebuttal to their vilification. His official biographer, Edgar C. McMechen, specifically names Thomas M. Patterson, owner of the *Rocky Mountain News* and *The Denver Times,* as among Speer's political foes. But the author maintains a discreet silence in regard to the Bonfils-Tammen attacks on Speer in *The Denver Post.*

Actually, it was a three-way dog fight. Both Patterson and Bonfils hated Speer, but they hated each other so much that it was a joke to find them on the same side of the fence. The mud-slinging in the columns of their papers reached a final pitch in December, 1907, when Patterson called Bonfils a "blackmailer." The day after Christmas, Bonfils saw Patterson strolling down from his Capitol Hill mansion to his newspaper office. Bon attacked the elderly, near-sighted editor with his fists, breaking Patterson's upper plate and bloodying his nose and cheeks. In retaliation,

Patterson had Bonfils arraigned in court and the testimony with regard to the *Post's* methods for obtaining advertisers gave the town some juicy tidbits.

But in 1904, both newspaper factions had stood together against Speer. The blond, distinguished-featured candidate for mayor had come to Colorado in 1878, as a twenty-three-year-old, hemorrhaging with tuberculosis. When he recovered sufficiently to take a job, he went to work for Daniels & Fisher Stores as a carpet salesman at $8 a week. The flying lint from the rugs irritated his lungs and he transferred to office work, first in private business and then in politics.

He was elected City Clerk in 1884, appointed Postmaster in 1885, and four years later, when the Republicans regained power, returned to the real estate business. Later, he served as City Police Commissioner, Fire Commissioner and President of the Board of Public Works. It was on his record in these three offices that the people of Denver, ignoring the blasts from the *News,* the *Times,* and the *Post,* gave him the mayoralty.

He was re-elected in 1908 and again in 1916, dying in office in 1918, at the age of sixty-two. No other single man stamped his imprint on the city as did this courageous, far-seeing man. And Speer, who never ceased to cherish a vision of a new and different Denver had to fight for his ideal in the face of constant and vindictive warfare.

The same election that first put Speer in power also gave the town a new charter and divorced Denver from Arapahoe County. The new mayor received autocratic powers which he began to use vigorously. The town that he ruled had a population of some one hundred-fifty thousand citizens; but it looked like an over-grown cow town—dusty, barren, and ugly. Speer wanted to make it beautiful.

He dreamed of parks, boulevards, fountains, statues, a civic auditorium and a civic center—all this external and visible—but, more importantly, he wanted the city sanitary and safe. To insure sanitation, two hundred and sixty-two miles of sewers were laid at a cost of close to three million dollars. Two hundred and thirteen miles of streets were graded and half that mileage, surfaced; sidewalks and curbings were extended on all sides. For the first time in its existence, Denver began to look tidy.

In his campaign for safety, he made war on the railroad magnates to force them to build the Twentieth Street viaduct. He threatened them with a city ordinance that would require each train to come to a full stop until signalled to proceed by a city watchman. The railroads were in the habit of buying troublesome city councils—they just smiled smugly and laughed off the upstart mayor.

Then, the railroads found they couldn't manipulate this council— a majority were Speer adherents. The council passed the ordinance, and the presidents of the railroads hurried around to a special session in the mayor's office. Angrily they demanded:

"You don't think the people of Denver will let you tie up through train service, do you?"

"The people of Denver probably think citizens' lives are more important. Actually, no one knows how the public will react, but I'm betting my way. The ordinance will be enforced."

Mayor Speer had a characteristic gesture of clenching his fist and banging it on the table to enforce a point, accompanied by a pet phrase. He used it now:

"There you have it, plunk!"

The railroads built the Twentieth Street viaduct at a cost of more than $600,000, of which the city's share was $66,000, a little over ten per cent. This episode illustrated Speer's forcefulness and his dedication to the people. The Colfax-Larimer viaduct was built in the 1912-1916 period, when he was out of office. It cost close to a million dollars and the city's share was around $850,000 in cash and city lots or eighty-five per cent. That other mayor had neither Speer's courage nor his sagacity.

On the score of beauty, the city of Denver remains a perpetual monument to Robert W. Speer. He began with Cherry Creek. In the very early days, it had one claim to prettiness—the cottonwood grove. But these trees were long since gone. The creek was a meandering mass of dried mud, rubbish and tin cans—a convenient city dump. Speer enclosed the wayward creek in concrete retaining walls and, on each side, built a boulevard which is now known by his name.

Other achievements followed. It was Frederick MacMonnies, sculptor of the Pioneer Monument at Colfax and Broadway, who first conceived the idea of a civic center. But Speer put it through. At that time, those blocks were a tangled assortment of apartment houses, residences and gimcrack business buildings. Speer started condemnation proceedings to get rid of them and to build the present sightly core of the town.

Today, nearly every park, statue, fountain and recreational development within the city, and, in addition, the Denver Mountain Parks system (one of the first systems of city-owned scenic and picnic acreage outside the city limits) and the Mt. Evans Drive are due to Speer. His love for Denver is manifest.

Perhaps his greatest contribution to Denver was a simple thing. The town lies on prairie land, land that is natively a waste of coarse buffalo grasses, prairie dog hills, cactus and tumbleweed.

"No town can be beautiful without trees," said Mayor Speer.

He inaugurated an annual tree day in April, 1905. Saplings were given away free to the citizens, who were requested to plant them along the parkings. That first year nearly five thousand tiny trees, their roots

CIVIC CENTER

The Voorhies Memorial with its sea lions, fountain and pool is on the north side of the Civic Center. It has murals by Allen True, sculpture by Robert Garrison; and cost a hundred and forty thousand dollars; left by the J. H. P. Voorhieses. It dates from 1922.

enclosed in gunny sacking, were donated to the people. The custom was continued until April, 1912, when on the last tree day eighteen thousand diminutive elms and maples were given away to become in time the stalwarts that now shade Denver streets.

Mayor Speer also loved green lawns and he ordered that every "Keep Off the Grass" sign, owned by the Parks Department, should be dumped in the ash can. To this day, Denver parks are open to the public's care-free enjoyment. One often sees entire families and their belongings spread out for a Sunday picnic, lovers strolling hand-in-hand, and children reveling in the turf. Denver's trees and lawns are a source of both pride and care. Each home owner has had to drag about heavy hoses and reset nozzles frequently to get the present effect of abundant greensward.

Most visitors to the arid West take water for granted. They comment pleasantly about the emerald color of Denver's lawns and think no more about it. But to Denver, water is the line between life and death. So important is this story that it has been recorded in the rotunda of the State Capitol in a series of eight murals, painted by Allen True and captioned by Thomas Hornsby Ferril with poetic couplets.

It was plain that if Denver was to grow, she must have water. The *Post* contributed one step in the solution of this problem by a crusade against the privately owned corporation, The Denver Water Company. Their crusade forced the city to buy out the company. Speer contributed another step when he reorganized the physical plant to conserve and efficiently use the Denver water supply.

But that supply was limited. The rainfall on the eastern slope of

SUMMER FUN

The captions on these two pages may seem transposed; but they do mean what they say. Skating is a major summer attraction both at the Denver University Arena and at the stockyards Coliseum. Eight or ten professionals offer a s p e c i a l ten-week program to coach amateurs in fancy figures. The public is cordially invited to watch.

the Rockies and every acre-foot of water it produced had long since been allocated to irrigation of lands along the Platte and Arkansas and to reservoirs of towns situated near the base of the mountains—Loveland, Boulder, Golden, Colorado Springs and Pueblo. Every drop of water was tagged long before it fell from a passing cloud. Denver's growth seemed doomed.

At the turn of the century, David Moffat was working on his transcontinental railroad dream. He wanted to build directly west from Denver to Salt Lake City and, in his preliminary plans, he visualized a two-and-a-half-mile tunnel through the Continental Divide. In 1889, he employed a young civil and mining engineer, George J. Bancroft, familiar with the James Peak terrain, to make auxiliary surveys and to give additional advice on the exact location of the bore. It was then that it occurred to Bancroft that a tunnel could carry something more than tracks through the mountains—namely, water.

In 1900, Bancroft and James Steele took mountain-wise ponies and a pack mule to investigate this possibility. They travelled the crest of the Continental Divide southwest from James Peak to Hoosier Pass to check on the feasibility of diverting Western Slope water to the eastern side of the range. As a result of this trip, filings were made on the Moffat Tunnel project, Berthoud Pass diversion, Vasquez Pass, Williams Fork project, and on the Blue River.

At the end of the trip, Bancroft suggested to Moffat the idea of using the "Pioneer Tunnel" for diverting water. The great Coloradan liked the idea and put up the money to finance Bancroft's filings and preliminary work. Moffat used his own money, since the water project was not an essential part of the railroad plan. Eventually, the Moffat Tunnel

WINTER WORK

Denver school children study in fine buildings, charmingly situated, because of Lucius Hallett, far-visioned, former school board president. Three bond issues were voted during 1919-1924 that totalled close to eleven million dollars. This is West High School and the Sunken Gardens near Cherry Creek on Speer Boulevard, taken in the autumn.

filings, together with all of Bancroft's other diversion filings, were transferred to the Denver Water Commission. The town's water problem was solved for years to come.

Denver heaved a sigh of relief and expanded as result. From 1900 to 1910 her population rose from 133,859 to 213,381, and in the next decade it reached 256,369. Mayor Speer and Water had made her look fresh and clean. Determined to be a clean city in every sense, in 1915 she shut up the sporting houses on Market Street. Then she settled back like a pleasantly satisfied matron—fair, fat and flourishing—to entertain her visiting friends and relatives.

This she continued to do. By 1940, her population had mounted to 332,412. She had a delightful climate, magnificent scenery, and all the requirements to become the center of a national playground. Gratefully, she accepted her role as a tourist town.

Only occasionally did a nostalgia for those rambunctious other days overcome her. In the '30s, the price of gold climbed to $35 an ounce and a renaissance of mining swept over the mountain camps. A few Denverites entered into the excitement but mostly the city remained complacent. Denver concentrated on ideas for the tourists—on renovating the Central City Opera House and starting a Pioneer Revival Festival there and on completing the Red Rocks Amphitheatre, whose setting had been hewn by nature from stupendous, rose red sandstone slabs.

There were occasional poignant reminders of her more romantic past— such as of Joe Potvin, known to all Denver as the "blind violet man." He was white-haired and always wore a broad-brimmed miner's Stetson while he tended a flower-vending stand on Curtis Street. As the theatre-

NEW HOMES

Monaco Parkway, near Twenty-second Street, is one of the many sections where Denver's fast-growing population is expanding into pretty modern residences.

goers hurried along Denver's former Gay White Way, he pled for purchasers with a monotonous "Roses and violets, roses and violets."

Nearly everyone who passed him knew that he had left his home in upstate New York to join in the Leadville rush; that he had staked out a claim in the Copper King mine and started development. There one night, as he was thawing some frozen dynamite on a stove in his cabin, it had exploded and blinded him. But the accident did not sour Potvin on mining. While he sold flowers night after night, he dreamed of the riches his mine would some day yield.

During the depression, Potvin looked more and more frail, and his plea sounded strained. In 1932, he was seventy-five years old and during the last few days he worked, he paid $1.50 for flowers that sold only 75c worth. Then suddenly his dream *did* come true. High grade ore was discovered in his mine and Potvin retired to "Easy Street." Occasionally, he sold flowers for something to do. In 1936 when he was nearly eighty years old, he went East and died on the trip.

Denver's last familiar link with her glamorous history was gone. The city honestly shed tears, not so much for Potvin as for the passing of the symbol, the violet vendor had presented nightly, of the unconquerable pioneer spirit—the kind of spirit that had originally made Denver.

But the nostalgic mood faded. After all, this was the twentieth century, mining was a thing of the past and Denver really had nothing to complain about. Perhaps her new role was not so dramatic, but the show in which she was playing promised to be a long-time run.

She settled back and smiled. Denver saw her name on the marquee as a great tourist town.

* * *

SIGHTS TO SEE

Contemporary Denver is engaged in another feud—whether the town should continue to be recreational or whether it should turn industrial. Recommendations to the visitor, as to what he should do and see, depend largely on which side of the creek his guide is on, whether in spirit he hails from Auraria or whether he prefers to join the go-getting promoters.

If he is of the first group, his viewpoint is pre-World War II. He is content with Denver as a tourist town and he prefers its former tempo, leisurely suited to a provincial podunk. His advice will be to hear a band concert in City Park, feed the ducks, watch the electric color fountain play, observe the statues, stroll through the museums, take a tour through the gold-bullioned Denver Mint, see the view from either the dome of the State Capitol or the top of the D. & F. Tower, attend a play at Elitch's, watch a boat race on Sloan's Lake or its lakeshore archery and trap shooting, and take a picnic lunch to enjoy a scenic day in Denver's Mountain Parks, where a herd of live buffalo grazes in Genessee Park and Buffalo Bill is buried on Lookout Mountain.

Particularly is he proud of Denver's park system. both within and without the city limits. It is unique, and offers such a wide variety of features that only a brief summary can be mentioned here. Picnic grounds will be found in all of the parks and bathing at most within the city. In the winter, these same lakes offer skating with the addition of Evergreen Lake, twenty-seven miles from Denver. Included in Denver's thirty parks and 22,000 acres is Winter Park which provides skiers with snow on different grade slopes and a helpful tow. There is a park for every taste.

If your guide prefers close-at-hand sports, his suggestions will be to drive north on Vasquez Boulevard to the Mile-High Kennel Club where there is pari-mutuel dog racing nightly and pick a quinella; to drive south on Santa Fe Drive to the Centennial Turf Club, where there is afternoon horse racing, and bet on the daily double; to see the Denver Bears of the recently revived Western league play baseball at their North Denver stadium; to attend the midget auto races at Lakeside Amusement Park; to gasp at the "hot rod" and stock car races on the Englewood Speedway; to catch a softball game on one of Denver's twelve lighted fields; to see the Colorado Open Tennis Tournament at the Country Club in July; to watch the figure skating at the Coliseum or at Denver University; or to play golf on one of Denver's five municipal golf courses (the historic Overland Park Golf Course is on the site of the original Montana Diggings and within "spitting" distance of a commemorative marker).

If he has artistic leanings, he will advise a thirty-five mile drive to hear fine opera in the quaint opera house at Central City, enlivened at intermission time by watching square dancing in a stable across the street,

CITY PARK

Three lakes, a pony farm, zoo, band tunes, pavilion, public motor launch, sportive fountains, many statues, gay planted flower beds and, of course, ever-hungry ducks, make the outdoors appealing to visitors.

or suggest a fifteen mile trip to listen to a symphony concert in the Red Rocks Amphitheatre. Both are rare experiences.

But if your guide is of the more modern group, those who are in hot pursuit of a commercial progress, he will be pleased that the 1950 census ranked Denver as twenty-fifth largest in the nation and that the town has had to install a complicated traffic system. He will tell you of Denver's enormous expansion in recent years and will point with pride to the Rocky Mountain Arsenal, the Air Force Finance Center, the atomic plant, the Veterans' Administration insurance center, Fitzsimons General Hospital for war wounded, the heavily scheduled air lanes leading in and out of Stapleton Field and a network of government offices of the Reclamation Bureau, housed on the site of a former small arms ordnance plant. He will tell you that all these combine to make bureaucratic Denver "The Washington of the West" and center of federal power for the region.

His suggestions will include taking a guided tour through the new plants of *The Denver Post* and *Rocky Mountain News* to see the great whirring presses, and dining in the Sky Chef Restaurant at the airport, where the fascination of the big aluminum birds, as they arrive and depart, gives a twentieth-century seasoning to the meals.

With such a plethora of offerings, the uninitiated tourist may easily be confused.

The practical solution to this dilemma is to go first to the Denver Hospitality Center, situated at 225 West Colfax (Route 40) just opposite the City and County Building. Here an efficient staff answers questions, gives out free literature and maps, and directs the bewildered tourist to all sorts of destinations—from where to get the carburetor on his engine attuned to high-altitude sparking, to where he can buy dry flies for trout fishing. Here is the spot to make decisions about sight-seeing.

SLOAN'S LAKE

Unique among Denver lakes is busy Sloan's, whose Mile High Boat Club has weekly races of thirty sail boats and a regatta, August 1. One hundred and sixty motorboats also race twice a year for sport.

Among pamphlets and folders that they offer for free distribution are a forty-page, year-round vacation pamphlet, "Come to Denver," Denver Hotels and Motels Guide, "Where to Eat in the Denver Area," City Map of Denver, Mountain Trips Folder, State Highway Map, Dude Ranch folders, Ski folders and reports, and luggage and auto stickers.

The Denver Chamber of Commerce at 1301 Welton Street or 1726 Champa has an even more extensive and elaborate list of free publications. These include "Denver, the Mile High City, "Distinctive Denver," "Industrial Denver," "Denver Labor," "Your Denver Vacation" and "Enjoy Health and Recreation in Denver." The Title Guaranty Company at 1711 California Street gives away a very interesting (although somewhat inaccurate) "Gems from Denver's Treasure Chest of History," remarkable for its old photographs. All these publications are lavishly illustrated.

Having picked up adequate material to make a choice, the conscientious sight-seer will certainly begin with the Civic Center and take a stroll about its grounds. The statues are not only worth viewing but have interesting stories connected with their erection. The most ornate is the Pioneer Group at Colfax and Broadway, which marks the end of the Smoky Hill route for crossing the plains in the gold rush days. That route was the most perilous and led to starvation, murder and even cannibalism. Frederick MacMonnies' statue pictures typical figures of the time.

The two figures which stand at each side of the entrance to the Greek Theatre, from the Civic Center, are of a cowboy and an Indian (see photo on page 4). They are called "Bucking Broncho" and "On the War Trail." The sculptor was A. Phimster Proctor of Los Altos, California, who had lived in Denver as a boy and attended the old Broadway school. They cost $17,500 each and were donated by J. K. Mullen and Stephen Knight,

AMPHITHEATRE

The Red Rocks open-air concerts are an unequalled experience for the sightseer. The natural Wagnerian setting is world-famed. The pueblo-type building at left is a fine restaurant, soda fountain and curio, souvenir and gift shop.

both admirers of Robert W. Speer and his dream of beautifying Denver. They were completed shortly after the great builder's death, in 1920 and in 1922.

A cowboy who was wanted for murder posed for the first, due to an understanding sheriff. Proctor had chosen his type and started his chiseling of the cowboy figure, when his subject shot an enemy. The sheriff, unlike most officers of the law, had an appreciation for art and stayed his hand until the statue was finished!

A Blackfoot, "Big Beaver," posed for the Indian figure and it is notable for the veracity of its portraiture.

On the Capitol side of the Civic Center, there is first "The Volunteer," standing at the front of the building in commemoration of the many Civil War heroes sent by the young territory of Colorado to the national struggle. It was sculptured by John D. Howland, an extraordinary figure of early times, who was an Indian fighter, a scout, a pioneer settler and one of the Denverites who took part in the famous battle of Glorieta Pass. The formal Civil War figure gives no hint of the adventurous life of its artist.

To the rear of the Capitol is "The Closing Era" by Preston Powers. The statue's title was suggested by John Greenleaf Whittier, while the statue itself was the gift of the artist who lived in Florence, Italy. For a short time in the early '90s, Powers was the art director of the University of Denver and worked on this statue. In 1893 a group of art patrons sent it to the World's Fair in Chicago as part of the Colorado exhibit. It was there that the poet-author of "Snowbound" saw the statue and suggested its title.

Having completed an inspection of the grounds, the visitor should tour all the buildings that bound the civic center, beginning with the Capitol Building. In the summer, attractive girl guides, dressed in cowgirl cos-

SKI COUNTRY

Two hours from Denver is the Continental Divide and some of the best skiing in America. These peaks are Cone, Flora, Witter, Eva, Bancroft and James as they look from one of Denver's Mountain Parks, Genesee Mountain.

tumes, conduct tours at regular intervals, starting from just inside the Colfax street entrance on the first floor. They also distribute a fine historical pamphlet giving the main facts about the state and the details of the state-owned buildings. From the dome of the building, the tourist will see one of the most magnificent views of the nation (photo on page 29). This is the Front Range of the Colorado Rockies.

For those who are interested in investigating the mountains at first hand, the State Publicity Office, Room 224, has an excellent pamphlet, "Cool, Colorful Colorado," giving descriptions of twelve round trips from Denver. It has maps and is illustrated with color photography.

The next building to be visited should be the State Museum at Fourteenth and Sherman, where the pictorial dioramas tell the history of the territory as no words can. Don't miss the West Hall, on the first floor.

Here is "The Model of Denver," an exact replica of the town in 1860, eleven by twelve feet in size, where the men on the sidewalks are less than half an inch high and the diminutive oxen and horses on the streets were cast in lead from carved wood originals. Indian Row with the Russell-McGaa double cabin, Uncle Dick Wootton's two-storied building, and all the familiar landmarks are there, exactly as it appeared to those who arrived in the second year of the Gold Rush.

Gazing down on the tiny town, it seems incredible that it was less than a hundred years ago that Denver looked like this—actually within the memory of a very few old-timers still alive today. Yet along those streets walked Kit Carson, the most fearless and trusted of early scouts. He probably marveled as much at what he saw then as we do, looking at the model. He could remember it as a far-away, lonely spot in the midst of wilderness through which, not too many years before, he had led the explorer, "Pathfinder" John C. Fremont.

MAMA GRIZZLY NO LONGER SEES THE FOUNTAIN PLAY

Louis Jonas' sculpture, the gift of John McGuire, former editor of "Outdoor Life," has been moved from this fine location of 1913-1951 to a poor position among the trees, but the cubs are still the delight of all children. This view also shows the horticultural pool, main City Park lake, electric fountain in the lake's center and the Pavilion. The Evans group of snow peaks and dark Squaw and Santa Fe are beyond.

Still another scout, more publicized than performing, knew the town when it was not much bigger than depicted in the model. He was Buffalo Bill (William F. Cody), who in later years was part of the Sells-Floto Circus, owned by Harry Tammen of *The Denver Post.* Buffalo Bill's "Wild West Show" toured the world and made Denver known to Europe more successfully than any other single factor. Today, Buffalo Bill lies in a grave on a foothill above the town that made him famous. A museum, close by, tells his story.

It is astounding to think that our grandfathers needed men like Kit Carson and Buffalo Bill to show them Denver and to protect them, at the same time, from many dangers. So fast has our century gone that all we need is the impulse to see the sights. Everything else has been made safe and easy.

So, at the model of Denver in 1860, we bid you adieu. In some ways, it is exactly the same feuding, individualistic town as it was then, and, in your sight-seeing, we leave you to find out just how and where.

SUGGESTIONS FOR FURTHER READING

Articles

DENVER, Levette J. Davidson. *Rocky Mountain Review*, Winter, 1945. A scholarly and fair-minded presentation by an English professor at the University of Denver.

DENVER, Robert Perkin and Charles A. Graham, in "ROCKY MOUNTAIN CITIES," a book edited by Ray B. West, Jr. A reporter on the *Rocky Mountain News* and a Denver lawyer who shared a liberal, vigorous viewpoint, collaborated to portray their home town in trenchant prose not afraid to call a spade by its right color.

DENVER, George Sessions Perry, in "CITIES OF AMERICA," a book composed of a series that originally appeared in the *Saturday Evening Post*. The author's style is pictorial; his reporting, much more accurate than other magazine contributions of the last decade.

Contemporary Books

HERE THEY DUG THE GOLD, George F. Willison. Lively history of early Colorado with a number of the chapters laid in Denver.

TIMBERLINE, Gene Fowler. The rollicking, sometimes raucous and fallacious, story of *The Denver Post* and its picturesque founders, Frederick G. Bonfils and Harry H. Tammen.

THE WILDEST OF THE WEST, Forbes Parkhill. The madams, the gamblers and the bunco-steerers frolic across these pages along with other unusual characters of Denver and Colorado history.

Formal Histories

HISTORY OF DENVER, Jerome C. Smiley. A monumental but entertaining volume, published in 1901, that is indispensable for any serious study of the town.

COLORADO AND ITS PEOPLE, edited by LeRoy R. Hafen. The latest and most comprehensive four volume history of the state with which Denver's destiny and progress are inextricably woven.

THE EARLY SETTLEMENTS OF DENVER, Nolie Mumey. Invaluable because of its fine illustrations and excellent reproductions of the first city directory, the 1859 map, the first issue of the *Rocky Mountain News* and the rare *Cherry Creek Pioneer*.

ACKNOWLEDGMENTS

For Research Aid:

As in all of my historical work, I want to thank the alert and unusual staff of the Western History Department of the Denver Public Library—Ina T. Aulls, Alys Freeze, Opal Harber and Louisa Ward Arps—who have been known to find needles in haystacks. At the Colorado State Museum, Agnes Wright Spring is always more than generous and Frances Shea and Mrs. James Harvey are recurrently obliging; as is Bob Canny at the *Post*.

For Criticism:

Marian Castle, distinguished author of "The Golden Fury," a pocketbook novel of Colorado's bonanza days that has sold over a million copies, is a constant foe of what she calls 'gobbledygook' in my early drafts. Her vigilant eye, her impeccable taste and her astute analysis have improved many a line in this manuscript and others 'born to blush unseen.'

For Proofreading:

Mrs. J. Alvin Fitzell catches many typographical errors with her bright blue eyes.

For Publicity Photographs:

Brown Palace Hotel, City of Denver Parks Department, Colorado Historical Society, Denver Art Museum, Denver Chamber of Commerce, Denver Hospitality Center, Denver Museum of Natural History, Denver and Rio Grande Railroad, Elitch's Gardens, University of Denver and the Windsor Hotel.